HINDUISM

HINDUISM

BY

L. D. BARNETT, M.A., D.Litt.

ASSISTANT IN THE DEPARTMENT OF ORIENTAL
PRINTED BOOKS AND MSS. OF THE
BRITISH MUSEUM

GYAN

Published by

GYAN

Gyan Publishing House
5, Ansari Road
Daryaganj, New Delhi-110002
Phone: 011-47034999, 9811692060
E-mail: books@gyanbooks.com

Distribution Network
gyanbooks.com
India, USA, Canada, UK, Australia, France

ISBN : 978-81-212-2720-9 (HB)
First Published, 1906

2nd Impression 2021

Printed at: Gyan Press, Delhi.

Hinduism
Author: L. D. Barnett

HINDUISM

By

L. D. BARNETT, M.A., D.Litt.

ASSISTANT IN THE DEPARTMENT OF ORIENTAL
PRINTED BOOKS AND MSS. OF THE
BRITISH MUSEUM

LONDON
ARCHIBALD CONSTABLE & CO Ltd
16 JAMES STREET HAYMARKET
1906

CONTENTS

HINDUISM

HINDUISM

Meaning of 'Hinduism.'—The term 'Hinduism' is one which we use for the sake of convenience to designate the religious creeds and practices of more than two hundred and seven millions of Hindus. These creeds and practices differ, in some cases slightly, in other cases immensely, from one another in their principles, and in the social principles with which they are organically connected; and this catholic variety, which has existed for about three thousand years and is still a marked feature of Hinduism, renders it singularly difficult to define the latter. Hinduism is not one homogeneous growth of religious thought; it is neither a single tree nor a forest of trees sprung from the same stock. It is, on the contrary, an aggregation of minor growths, some of cognate origin, some of foreign provenance, all grouped under the shadow of one mighty tree. It is an influence which has taken possession of wellnigh all the roads by which man approaches the Unseen in India; its churches are as well the stately cathedral where scholars and princes worship as the humble shrine where villagers offer wild flowers to some god born of their own rude hearts, or the wayside spot haunted by some random godling who may have dwelt there long before Hindus came into India, or may have arrived there last week. Over all these provinces Hinduism wields empire, or at least suzerainty.

The kernel of Hinduism consists of two groups of ideas. The first of these is the conception of a social order, or caste-system, at the head of which stand the Brahmans as completest incarnation of the Godhead and authoritative exponents of Its revelation. Secondly, we have a series of ideas which may be summed up in three words—'Works' (*karma*), 'Wandering' (*saṃsāra*), and 'Release' (*moksha*). This means that life—*i.e.* the finite experience of the soul—is a curse; the infinitely many souls which make up the sum of the universe wander in repeated incarnation from body to body, now higher, now lower, every instant of their experience being the direct resultant of some previous act, and itself resulting in a future act, and thus reaching backwards and forwards to infinity; so long as there remains attached to the soul a positive resultant of this infinite series of works, the soul is 'fettered,' doomed to continued birth in body; only a few elect souls in which the resultant finally vanishes attain everlasting emancipation, which, according to some schools, consists in absorption in the absolute All-Being, *Brahma,* and according to others is union therewith.

Hinduism then denotes all provinces of thought in which all or most of these ideas are at least nominally accepted. At its centre are the great systems in which they are fully acknowledged; at its extremities stand in ill-defined dependence a number of minor churches which hardly admit them at all, especially the claims of the Brahmans. The elasticity of these common links is so great that some writers have sought other definitions of Hinduism, and one has described it as 'Animism more or less transformed by philosophy,' or 'magic tempered by metaphysics'; 'at one end, at the lower end of the series, is Animism, an essentially materialistic theory of things which seeks by means of magic to ward off or to forestall physical disasters, which looks no further than the world of sense, and seeks to make that as tolerable as the conditions will permit. At the other end is Pantheism combined with a system of transcendental metaphysics.'[1]

Animism as an unlettered mode of worship is treated in a separate volume of this series. The present book seeks mainly to give a brief account of the chief systems in which the religious thought of India has found literary utterance.

The Vedic Age.—The oldest document of Indian religion, and indeed of Aryan religion in general, is the *Rig-veda*, or 'Lore of the Verses,' a collection of hymns to various gods which were composed for the worship of the Aryan tribes invading India during the earlier centuries of their dwelling in the land, about 1000 B.C., while they were still far up in the North-West. Some of the deities thus worshipped are simply forces of nature, over whose purely physical character the poets cast only a thin veil of allegory and metaphor. Such are Father Heaven (*Dyaus-pitā*, the Greek *Zeus patēr*) and Mother Earth (*Pṛithivī*, the Greek *Gaia Mētēr*), the Dawn-goddess *Ushas* (Gr. *Ēōs*), the Sun-god *Sūrya* (Gr. *Hēlios*), the Wind-god *Vāyu*. With other deities new attributes and trains of ideas have been connected which tend to obscure their original

[1] *Census of India*, 1901, vol. i. p. 357.

character. Thus the very popular god *Agni*, whose name means 'fire,' personifies the earthly fire of ritual and domestic use, the atmospheric fire of lightning, and sometimes even the sun in the heavens; and he becomes the priest, the seer, mediating between man and gods. Another god is *Indra*, who seems originally to have typified the stormy atmospheric forces whose most striking manifestation is the thunderbolt, being in fact a *Ζεὺς τερψικέραυνος*; but a vast amount of myth of all kinds has attached itself to this figure, which naturally had a strong fascination for the fierce fancy of the warlike Aryans, and at length became their favourite god. Another great deity is *Varuṇa*, who seems to have at first typified the open sky, whose eye is the sun, and thence has grown into a mighty guardian of the laws of nature and morality.

A very interesting Vedic god is *Soma*. He is the spirit of the *soma*-plant (now unknown), the juice of which, being intoxicating, was accounted divine.[1] The *soma*-juice, collected in vats from the bruised stalks, was copiously drunk by worshippers and offered to the gods; Indra was thought to be especially fond of it, as was natural

[1] In the same way Bacchus or Dionysus is simply the intoxicating 'spirit' of the fermented juice of the grape.

in a deity of his fiery character.[1] Under the influence of the *soma*, Indra, among other heroic deeds, slew the snaky monster Vṛitra and released the kine (probably a metaphor for the rain-clouds) penned up by him. The god Soma came to be connected in popular fancy with the moon, and was in the end completely identified with it.[2]

A few examples of the Vedic mode of utterance may be quoted.[3] Ushas is thus addressed (vii. 75):—

Born in the heavens the Dawn hath flushed, and showing her majesty is come as Law ordaineth,
She hath uncovered fiends and hateful darkness; best of Angirases, hath waked the pathways.
Rouse us this day to high and happy fortune: to great felicity, O Dawn, promote us.
Vouchsafe us manifold and splendid riches, famed among mortals, man-befriending Goddess!
See, lovely Morning's everlasting splendours, bright with their varied colours, have approached us.
Filling the region of mid-air, producing the rites of holy worship, they have mounted.
She yokes her chariot far away, and swiftly visits the lands where the Five Tribes are settled,

---

[1] Compare the ale-bibbing gods of the Scandinavians, who, like all deities, are but a glorified reflexion of their worshippers.

[2] The moon is always the patron or patroness of sorcerers; in India it is likewise the source of the sap of all vegetation.

[3] These are taken from Mr. Griffith's translation of the Ṛig-veda (Benares, 1897).

Looking upon the works and ways of mortals, Daughter of Heaven, the world's Imperial Lady.
She who is rich in spoil, the Spouse of Sûrya, wondrously opulent, rules all wealth and treasures.
Consumer of our youth, the seers extol her : lauded by priests rich Dawn shines out refulgent.
Apparent are the steeds of varied colour, the red steeds carrying resplendent Morning,
On her all-lovely car she comes, the Fair One, and brings rich treasure for her faithful servant.
True with the True and Mighty with the Mighty, with Gods a Goddess, Holy with the Holy,
She brake strong fences down and gave the cattle : the kine were lowing as they greeted Morning.
O Dawn, now give us wealth in kine and heroes, and horses, fraught with manifold enjoyment.
Protect our sacred grass from man's reproaches. Preserve us evermore, ye Gods, with blessings.

Varuṇa is thus addressed in a strain almost of monotheism (i. 25):—

Whatever law of thine, O God, O Varuṇa, as we are men,
Day after day we violate,
Give us not as a prey to death, to be destroyed by thee in wrath,
To thy fierce anger when displeased.

* * * * *

He knows the path of birds that fly through heaven, and, Sovran of the sea,
He knows the ships that are thereon.
True to his holy law, he knows the twelve moons with their progeny :
He knows the moon of later birth.[1]

---

[1] The intercalary month.

He knows the pathway of the wind, the spreading, high, and mighty wind:
He knows the Gods who dwell above.
Varuṇa, true to holy law, sits down among his people; he,
Most wise, sits there to govern all.
From thence perceiving he beholds all wondrous things, both what hath been,
And what hereafter will be done.

As a specimen of the many addresses to Indra the following will serve (i. 80):—

Thus in the Soma, in wild joy the Brahman hath exalted thee:
Thou, mightiest, thunder-armed, hast driven by force the Dragon from the earth, lauding thine own imperial sway.
The mighty flowing Soma-draught, brought by the Hawk, hath gladdened thee,
That in thy strength, O Thunderer, thou hast struck down Vṛitra from the floods, lauding thine own imperial sway.
Go forward, meet the foe, be bold; thy bolt of thunder is not checked.
Manliness, Indra, is thy might: slay Vṛitra, make the waters thine, lauding thine own imperial sway.
Thou smotest Vṛitra from the earth, smotest him, Indra, from the sky.
Let these life-fostering waters flow attended by the Marut host, lauding thine own imperial sway.

So the hymns run on endlessly. Another (vi. 45) begins thus:—

That Indra is our youthful Friend, who with his trusty guidance led
Turvaṣa, Yadu from afar.

Even to the dull and uninspired Indra gives vital power, and
    wins
Even with slow steed the offered prize.
Great are his ways of guiding us, and manifold are his
    eulogies:
His kind protections never fail.
Friends, sing your psalm and offer praise to him to whom the
    prayer is brought:
For our great Providence is he.

These Vedic poet-preachers have an inveterate propensity to assimilate different gods one to another because of some point of resemblance. Hence, since many gods were alike, a worshipper courting the favour of any deity felt little scruple in ascribing to him supremacy over all the others, whoever he might be. So the outlines of the divine forms became blurred, and faded away from the vision of thoughtful men, and the conception of an All-God, the pantheistic idea, grew clearer to them.

Passing over the rest of the numerous Vedic pantheon, we note two minor deities, Rudra and Vishṇu. Rudra seems to have originally typified the storm. He is a deity of a kind frequent in low civilisations, by nature malevolent and harmful, but capable if propitiated of bringing health and weal. Vishnu, on the other hand, typifies the journeying sun; he is a gracious deity, a worker for the powers of right and divine order.

The world of Vedic religion swarmed with gods (the number is usually given as thirty-three), with godlings and demons, and with the countless creations of fancy that spring up everywhere in an early state of culture saturated with animistic notions of godhead. This lower stratum of ideas is most prominent in the collection of hymns originally called *Atharvāngirasa*, and afterwards *Atharva-veda*, which now ranks as a fourth Veda with the Ṛig-veda and its two ritual recensions, the *Sāma-veda*, or 'Lore of the Chants,' and the *Yajur-veda*, or 'Lore of the Sacrifices.'

The dead were usually burned together with sacrifices, robes, ornaments, etc.[1] The spirits of the righteous pass to the abodes of the Fathers, a place of everlasting light in the highest heavens, the home of Vishṇu. Here they enjoy every imaginable delight of the senses, freed from all frailties of the body. Their ruler here is Yama, the first of men who lived and died. For the wicked Vedic belief seems to have created a gloomy hell.

[1] There is some evidence that widows were once burned with their lords' corpses. If so, the custom was discontinued; its revival is comparatively modern.

Vedic ritual was simple, as was natural in a community still young in civilisation. Each household had its altars, or rather trenches, containing the sacred fires, in which sacrifices were offered. For special occasions of sacrifice the householder hired a poet to compose a hymn which should gratify the deity concerned. A peculiar class of religious poets and priests was beginning to arise, and by the end of the Vedic age, about 800 B.C., this had grown into the Brahman caste claiming especial affinity with Godhead.

The Beginnings of Classical Hinduism.—As the Aryans spread their empire over India, the ghostly influence of the Brahmans increased. In their hands Vedic religion underwent a profound change. The divisions of the four great castes (*Brahmans*; *Kshatriyas*, or warriors; *Vaiśyas*, or traders; and *Śūdras*, or serfs) were mapped out in rigid demarcation. Most of the old Vedic gods remained, but they were not as they were before; for as the ideas of Pantheism rose on the mental horizon, the gods sank from an absolute to a relative immortality, Indra becoming the king of Paradise, Varuṇa the Lord of the Ocean. From them might however be won blessings in the worlds of sensuous life—and won by ritual;

and to this end the Brahmans now devoted their chief energies. The hymns of the Veda, supposed to be a divine revelation (*śruti*, 'hearing') vouchsafed to their composers, were regarded with ever-increasing veneration, as containing the principles alike of sacrificial practice and of philosophic speculation. The idea of sacrifice grew to an enormous degree, and, connoting as it did the spiritual supremacy of the Brahmans in every sphere, laid a crushing incubus upon the whole of Indian life. The entire weal of the world was imagined to depend upon the sacrificial ritual, the key of which was in the hands of the Brahmans. To this end were compiled, about 800 B.C., the *Brāhmaṇas*, huge works expounding and commenting upon the ritual application of the Vedic texts and the liturgies in general. Of the four great schools connected with the four Vedas (p. 10), each had a Brāhmaṇa of its own.

As typical of early Brahmanic ritualism we may mention two sacrifices which theoretically stand at the summit of their system, the *aśva-medha* and the *purusha-medha*. The *aśva-medha* was performed by kings to ensure the welfare and extension of their realms; amidst extremely elaborate and prolonged ceremonies a horse was choked, and an enormous number of smaller animals slain with it. It was currently believed that a hundred of such sacrifices would enable a king to depose Indra from his throne in heaven. Still more potent was the *purusha-medha*, where a man was made to take the place of the horse. In practice, no doubt, both of these rites were rare; but they were certainly real. In this Golden Age of Brahmanism priestcraft reigned supreme, ingeniously silly and bloodily sanctimonious; and though the priesthood in the course of time have learned mercy and charity, they have indemnified themselves by preserving and glorifying the obscenities of the folk-religions of which they made themselves guardians.[1]

The Brahmanic schools however contained something better than ritualism. The latest hymns of the Ṛig-veda preach in a tentative way an elementary Pantheism. The Brahmans carried on these speculations further, until at length they emerge as trains of complete pan-

[1] The frailties of earth are in India translated to heaven with a frequency and boldness that would make even an Alexandrine Greek shudder. In many temples, both of Śiva and of Vishṇu, not to speak of minor gods, the plastic art is degraded to depict scenes that no English pen dare adumbrate. This does not necessarily imply vice in the worshippers' lives; but its influence on the moral fibre in general may be guessed.

theistic ideas, side by side with mystic fantasies on ritual, in the older *Upanishads*, or 'Sessions' (sixth or seventh century B.C.), which form appendices to the *Āraṇyakas*, or 'forest-books,' the later and more speculative sections of the Brāhmaṇas.[1]

Indian orthodoxy regards Vedas, Brāhmaṇas, Āraṇyakas, and Upanishads as alike divinely inspired Vedas, *Śruti*; and from them, and especially from the Upanishads, all the orthodox systems of metaphysics profess to derive their authority. And indeed the importance of the Upanishads in the religious and philosophic history of India can hardly be exaggerated. In them are definitely set forth, almost for the first time, the doctrines of 'Work' and 'Wandering of Souls,' which, as we saw (p. 2), are the pillars of Hinduism. The Upanishads are indeed far from being consistent and systematic. But the older Upanishads—as distinct from the majority of the tracts forming the modern canon, which are mostly sectarian and much later—agree in their general principle, which is, in brief, that the essence of all being is the One absolute Being, *Brahma* (neuter), or 'Supreme Self' (*Para-*

[1] The purely ritualistic side of the Brāhmaṇas also developed a logical method in the *Pūrva-mīmāṃsā* schools.

mātmā), unconditioned Thought, with which the individual soul or 'Self' (*Ātmā*) is identical, as microcosm with macrocosm, being restrained from consciousness of its unity, and hence from union, by the resultants of its previous 'Works.' The knowledge and quietism of the Brahman saint are the only way to this salvation.

The spirit of Upanishadic Pantheism is pithily summed up in 'Śāṇḍilya's Lore' (Chhāndogya Upanishad, iii. § 14):—

Brahma in sooth is this All. It hath therein its beginning, end, and breath; so one should worship it in stillness.

Now Man in sooth is made of Will. As is Man's will in this world, so doth he become on going hence. Will shall he frame.

Made of mind, bodied of breath, revealed in radiance, true of purpose, ethereal of soul, all-working, all-loving, all-smelling, all-tasting, grasping this All, speaking naught, heeding naught, this my Self within my heart is tinier than a rice-corn or a barley-corn or a mustard-seed or a canary-seed or the pulp of a canary-seed. This my Self within my heart is greater than earth, greater than sky, greater than heaven, greater than these worlds.

All-working, all-loving, all-smelling, all-tasting, grasping this All, speaking naught, heeding naught, this is my Self within my heart, this is Brahma, to Him shall I win on going hence. He that hath this thought hath indeed no doubt.

Equally characteristic is the language of the Bṛihad-āraṇyaka Upanishad, chapter iv.:—

A narrow, far-drawn, old-time path to me-ward,
this I in sooth have found, whereon the Wise,
that wot the way of Brahma, wandering forth
in full enlargement, hence to heaven uprise.

* * * * *

Whoso shall find him the awaken'd Self,
that lodgeth in this darkling patch'd-up house,
builder of all is he, the All he maketh;
his is the world, the world in sooth is he.

When straightway he beholdeth god in Self,
sovran of what hath been and is to be,
his thought no more shall waver in its way.

Undying I and learned, so I deem
Brahma and deathless is that Self wherein
abide the Ether and the Orders five.

The gods do worship to the Light of Lights,
the everlasting Life, beyond whose bourn
rolleth the restless year its tale of days.

Who knoweth Breath of Breath and Sight of Sight,
Hearing of Hearing and the Food of Food,
who knoweth Mind of Mind, hath understanding
of Brahma everlasting, set on high,
Mind shewing that naught manifold is here.

He winneth death of death who seeth here
a Manifold. By Mind there cometh sight
of this unaging everlasting One.

Undimmed, beyond the ether, and unborn,
mighty and everlasting is the Self.
This known, wise Brahmans gather understanding,
nor feed their thought upon a many words;
for this is but a weariness of speech.

This Self is master of all, lord of all, King of all, ruleth over all this that is. By a good deed he groweth not greater, neither by an ill deed less. He is king of born beings, lord of the worlds, warden of the worlds, the dyke holding asunder these worlds so that they burst not one upon another. . . .

The Self is 'No, No!' Not to be grasped, it is not grasped; not to be broken, it is not broken; unclinging, unbound, it clingeth not; it wavereth not. Therefore the deathless one passeth alike beyond the thought of his sinful works and beyond the thought of his godly works. Good and evil, work done and work undone, grieve him not. By no work whatsoever is the world lost to him.

Thereon a verse tells:

> The Brahman's biding might nor waxeth more
> nor waneth by his works. This shall he learn;
> the learned deeds of ill no more befoul.

Obviously there is a practical deficiency in this scheme. It gives little scope for the true religious sense. It admits indeed gods—the Demiurge *Brahmā* (masculine), variously styled also *Prajāpati* and *Hiraṇyagarbha*, as well as Vedic gods such as Indra and Varuṇa—but none of these are absolutely immortal or able to command the full allegiance of heart and intellect from any worshipper, save the strict ritualist or the strict metaphysician. A supreme personal God was needed, whose figure should body forth to the mind's eye qualities claiming devout awe and love. Such deities were found in Śiva and Vishṇu, whose cults have ever since divided India into two rival churches.

The Cult of Vishṇu.—Vishṇu is already in the Ṛig-veda a god of grace (p. 9), and even in the Brāhmaṇas there is a growing tendency to regard him as a blessed Cosmic Spirit. Outside the pale of strict Brahmanic orthodoxy the cult of Vishṇu as supreme adorable God grew apace, until its claims to Brahmanic sanction could no longer be denied. Vishṇu was now acknowledged by many Brahmans as the absolute 'Supreme Self,' as the individual Self, and as the highest principle and essence of cosmic life (called in this capacity also *Nārāyaṇa* and *Hari*). Moreover, as his worship spread and absorbed many minor cults, it developed thence the idea of *avatars* (*avatāra*, 'descent'), *i.e.* incarnations of a larger or smaller portion of the divine spirit in human or animal form from age to age in order to maintain the order of righteousness in the world.[1]

[1] The incarnations most popular in modern Hinduism are (1) the *Fish*, which saved from the deluge Manu, the parent of mankind; (2) the *Tortoise*, which stood in the 'Ocean of Milk' and supported on its back Mount Mandara, with which the gods and demons churned the ocean and thence drew certain mythological treasures; (3) the *Boar*, which destroyed a demon

In this worship of Vishṇu there appeared a new element in Indian religion—faith or devotion, *bhakti*. So strong was this current that in many aspects of the cult it has entirely overshadowed its intellectual elements, and has sometimes led to the wildest debaucheries of religious emotion.

The Legend of Rāma.—This myth was one of the many absorbed by the conquering Vishṇuite church, and was early made the theme of a great epic, the *Rāmāyaṇa*, ascribed to the poet Vālmīki.[1] The Rāmāyaṇa narrates the birth of Rāma or Rāma-chandra (embodying half the divine essence), and of his half-brothers, Bharata, Lakshmaṇa, and Śatrughna, all of them sons of King Daśaratha of Ayodhyā (near the modern Faizabad); how in his early youth Rāma bent the ponderous bow of King of Janaka Videha (Mithilā),

and raised the submerged earth from the sea; (4) the *Man-lion*, which saved the pious youth Prahlāda by slaying his cruel father the demon Hiraṇya-kaśipu; (5) the *Dwarf*, who deposed the demon Bali from the dominion of the three worlds; (6) *Paraśu-rāma*, the Brahman hero, who destroyed the Warrior caste; (7) *Rāma*, or *Rāma-chandra*; (8) *Kṛishṇa*; (9) *Buddha*, in order to lure the impious to destruction by the sophistries of Buddhism; and (10) *Kalki*, an incarnation yet to come, in which Vishṇu will appear on a white horse with a drawn sword, to restore the order of righteousness. Every sectarian leader is worshipped by his sect as an incarnation of his favourite god.

[1] The nucleus of the poem was composed about 500 B.C., but it has been later recast and expanded.

and won as prize Janaka's daughter Sītā as his bride; how Rāma, exiled by his father, dwelt with Sītā and Lakshmaṇa in the woodlands, whence Sītā was carried off by the demon king Rāvaṇa to Lankā (Ceylon); how Rāma, aided by the hosts of the monkey-king, invaded Lankā, destroyed Rāvaṇa and his armies, and brought back Sītā to Ayodhyā, where he was crowned as king; how Rāma, moved by the foolish gossip of his people, sent Sītā away to the hermitage of Vālmīki. where she bore his two sons Kuśa and Lava; and how at length after reunion they were raised to heaven. The story is truly epic, and has an immense influence over the hearts of India, as indeed it deserves. It is read in some version in every village, and it has been made especially the Bible of the Hindi-speaking world by the noble poem of Tulsī Dās (sixteenth century).

The Legends of Kṛishṇa-Vāsudeva.—These are no less important in Vishṇuite worship than the story of Rāma. Originally it is possible that Kṛishṇa and Vāsudeva were different figures, which have been united and incorporated in the Vishṇuite cult. The chief literary sources are the *Mahābhārata* with its appendix the *Harivaṃśa*, the *Pāncharātra*, and the *Bhāgavata-purāṇa*.

The Mahābhārata is a gigantic collection which

began about 500 B.C. as an epic poem commemorating the wars of the Bhāratas (for whom afterwards the Pāṇḍavas were substituted) and the Kauravas; but this original form has been recast and expanded by additions of almost every conceivable kind of matter. In the older parts of the poem Kṛishṇa figures simply as a demigod and king; but in the later portions he is represented as the full incarnation of Vishṇu, especially in the *Bhagavad-gītā*, the most powerful and popular exposition of this aspect of the cult.

According to the legend, Kṛishṇa (so-called from his black or blue skin) was born as the son of Vāsudeva, and was saved from the murderous hands of Kaṃsa, king of Mathurā, by his father, who gave him into the charge of a herdsman, Nanda. Kṛishṇa spent his childhood and youth as a shepherd in Vraja (in Muttra District) about Vṛindāvana; and around this period of his life, and especially around his amours with Rādhā and the Gopīs, or herdswomen, a cycle of brilliantly sensuous myths has gathered, which seem hardly known in the Mahābhārata; the most popular record of them is the Bhāgavata-purāṇa.[1]

[1] A considerable number of the details in the Puranic myths of Kṛishṇa's birth and childhood seem to have come from debased Christian sources (apocryphal Gospels and the like) such as were current in the Christian church of Malabar.

Two of the oldest divisions of the Kṛishṇa-Vāsudeva cult are the schools called *Bhāgavatas* and *Pāncharātras* (or *Sātvatas*). The chief tenets of the former are preserved in the Bhāgavata-purāṇa. The doctrines of the latter are contained in the 108 *āgamas* collectively styled *Pāncharātra*; they were for the most part adopted and scholastically systematised by Rāmānuja (p. 31). With these schools the doctrine of the Bhagavad-gītā is closely allied.

The Bhagavad-gītā is a work of the boldest eclecticism. It begins by setting forth the Upanishadic psychology; it links this with the purely Vishṇuite theology by declaring the original unity of all souls with the Supreme Soul or Self represented as Vishṇu or his manifestation Kṛishṇa. Taking up the Sāṃkhya-Yoga antithesis of Soul and Matter, it puts Vishṇu above both as their primal source; it attempts to adjust the rival claims of Works and Knowledge, not very successfully, by preaching the duty of man to do the duties of his station in a spirit of perfect renunciation and devotion to Vishṇu, Kṛishṇa, or whatever the name in which the Supreme is proclaimed. This brings it into the sphere of genuine Vishṇuite *bhakti*, loving devotion to the personal God, with its usual accompaniment, the doctrine of 'special grace.' Thus it announces (xviii. 56-58)—

Doing always all works, making his home in Me, one attains by My grace to the everlasting changeless region.

Casting off with thy mind all works upon Me, be thou given over to Me; turned to Rule of the understanding, keep thy thought ever on Me.

If thou hast thy thought on Me, thou shalt by My grace pass over all hard ways; but if from thought of the *I* thou hearken not, thou shalt be lost.

The Cult of Śiva.—While Vishṇu is the Preserver, the loving guardian of all his creatures amidst the ceaseless change of cosmic life, *Śiva*, the Rudra of the Vedas (p. 9), 'represents . . . the earliest and universal impression of Nature upon men—the impression of endless and pitiless change. He is the destroyer and rebuilder of various forms of life; he has charge of the whole circle of animated creation, the incessant round of birth and death in which all Nature eternally revolves. His attributes are indicated by symbols emblematic of death and of man's desire; he presides over the ebb and flow of sentient existence. In Śiva we have the condensation of the two primordial agencies, the striving to live and the forces that kill. . . . He exhibits by images, emblems, and allegorical carvings the whole course and revolution of Nature, the inexorable law of the alternate triumph of life and death—*Mors janua Vitæ*—the unending circle of indestructible animation.'[1]

Śiva ('gracious one') or *Mahādeva* ('great god') is in essence the same as the Vedic Rudra —the god of the wild mountains. Fierce and terrible (whence his title *Bhairava*), he dwells with his bride Pārvatī in the heart of the Himalaya, attended by goblin bands, often amidst wild revelry. To symbolise the reproductive changes of nature, he has for token the *linga*, or male organ of generation; and as lord of the spirits of the dead he haunts graveyards, wearing garlands of serpents and a necklace of skulls. In a somewhat milder aspect, he appears as a *Yogī* or ascetic saint buried in millennial reverie, typical of the Hindu ascetics who seek by mortifications and abstraction of thought to attain supernatural powers and final union of the soul with the Absolute Spirit.

But horror and even grotesqueness of representation do not prevent an Indian god from winning intense personal love and devotion from his worshippers. As Vishṇu in his hideous idol

[1] Sir A. Lyall, *Asiatic Studies*, second series, p. 306.

at Puri (the famous Jagannāth) and elsewhere, so Śiva in all his legendary ugliness—naked, blue of throat and red of skin, or livid white, three-eyed, besmeared with ashes of cow-dung—is often invested by devout and refined imaginations with attributes of supreme sweetness and love.

The Trinity.—Usually the Demiurge *Brahmā*, who creates the universe, is claimed by either the Śaiva or the Vaishṇava church as an emanation of either Śiva or Vishṇu. But from time to time, doubtless under the influence of Upanishadic monism, an attempt had been made to resolve these claims in a Trinity wherein the three are one and the one three. This is illustrated, *e.g.* in a rock-carving at Elephanta, in which three heads arise from one body. But this conception has not penetrated deep into the religious consciousness. To the vast mass of Hindus the highest source of all existence is either Śiva or Vishṇu, in some form. Vaishṇavas regard Śiva and other gods as emanations of Vishṇu, and Śaivas view Vishṇu and the rest as sprung from Śiva.

The Śākta Cult.—Closely connected with the cult of Śiva is the worship of his wife (*Umā, Pārvatī, Gaurī, Tārā, Kālī, Durgā*, or *Mahādevī*) as *Sakti*, the cosmic energy or principle of determined life in the universe, in contrast to the absolute Being symbolised by Śiva as the Male.[1] The origin of this cult is no doubt to be sought in the matriarchal conditions of some of the more debased communities of the north. Its nature commended it to the sensuous mind revelling in ideas of lust and horror, its pseudo-philosophic explanation to the half-educated, and consequently it has spread deeply into Indian thought. Its followers are of two schools. The 'Walkers in the Right Way' (*dakshiṇāchārī*) pay a service of devotion to the deity in both male and female aspects, and, except in their more pronounced tendency to dwell upon the horrific aspects of the deity (as Kālī, Durgā, etc.), they differ little from ordinary Śaivas and Vaishṇavas. The 'Walkers in the Left Way' (*vāmāchārī*), on the other hand, concentrate their thought upon the godhead in its sexually maternal aspect, and follow rites of senseless magic and—theoretically at least—promiscuous debauchery. The *Tantras*, a series of comparatively modern compositions, contain the chief doctrines and rituals of the Śakti cult in its various forms.

Buddhism and Jainism.—The great currents of Śivaite and Vishṇuite thought, as we saw, pro-

[1] This cult has found its way into the Vishṇuite church also, but has not penetrated far.

foundly modified the severely metaphysical and ritualistic rigour of Brahmanisn. They even weakened the social position of the Brahmans, for they introduced the conception of the equality of all worshippers (though not necessarily of all men) in the eyes of their god. The way was now paved for a great reformation. A number of popular movements arose about the sixth century B.C., chiefly led by thinkers of the Warrior caste (*Kshatriya*). The greatest of these movements were Buddhism and Jainism. These two systems possess some common features. Firstly, they assert the sanctity of *all* life and hence the sinfulness of animal sacrifice; and to this they were moved by the now universal belief in the incarnation of souls in every kind of living thing, as well as simple repugnance to the butcherly ritualism of the Brahmans. Secondly, they claimed for their churches lineages of divinely inspired apostles of the Warrior caste, thus standing for the spiritual rights of the laity as against Brahmanic pretensions; and in the metaphysical side of their theology they were in close touch with the Sāṃkhya school, which, though formally claimed for Brahmanic orthodoxy, was really atheistic, entirely denying a supreme God.[1]

[1] See further the Appendix.

The position of the Brahmans, though shaken by these assaults, was in the end maintained. Gradually the older churches permeated the new communities with their ideas, and wore off the asperities of their opposition. In this way Jainism was slowly brought to its present attitude of moderate dissent, and Buddhism disappeared from the Indian continent, swallowed up by Śākta and Tantric cults. But they left their mark upon the general complexion of Indian religion, which has since shown a singular tenderness for life and sympathy with suffering in every sphere. Much of this change is doubtless due ultimately to Vishṇuite influence; but that it was so effectually carried out is certainly due to the aggressive nonconformity of the Buddhists, Jains, and cognate churches.

The Purāṇas.—In carrying on its long struggle with these rivals, Brahmanism found an effective instrument of propaganda in the *Purāṇas.* These are poems, usually of great length, and in simple popular style, recounting legends of the cosmogony, and myths of various kinds, chiefly of the cult of Vishṇu,[1] together with a vast amount

[1] The chief of them are the Agni, Bhāgavata, Bhavishya, Bhavishyottara, Brahma, Brahmāṇḍa, Brahma-vaivarta, Garuḍa, Kūrma, Linga, Mārkaṇḍeya, Matsya, Nārada, Padma, Śiva, Skanda, Vāmana, Varāha, Vāyu, and Vishṇu Purāṇas.

of most miscellaneous encyclopædic matter. Being intended for the spiritual benefit of the unlettered classes and the women, they present Brahmanic myth and doctrine in its most popular form, in its most exaggerated and grotesque aspects. Every available legend is pressed into the service of their deity, and every possible colour in which he can be painted so as to attract the vulgar imagination is laid on in monstrous profusion. The kernel of some of the Purāṇas is very ancient; but most of their matter was composed in the first ten centuries of our era, and they are still growing.

Śankara and the Vedānta.—Brahmanism, however, was now active in other fields also. The theories of pantheistic monism or *Advaita* developed in the Upanishads (p. 14) had been actively studied by many Brahman schoolmen, and one now arose who fixed the bases on which the philosophy and religion of the great majority of Hindus have ever since stood. This was Śankara Āchārya, a Malabar Brahman who lived about the ninth century. He completed and systematised the Upanishadic monism; and the word *Vedānta*, properly signifying the Upanishads themselves, is now commonly applied to his interpretation of them. The most remarkable feature of his system,[1] as compared with the older schools, is the theory of *Māyā*, 'jugglery' or 'illusion.' To earlier philosophers the universe is essentially a single *reality*, though veiled by the unessential plurality of phenomena; but to Śankara it is entirely *unreal* and illusive, born of a demiurgic power which is purely an 'accident' in the nature of the Absolute Brahma. The supreme Knowledge, as it were, imposes upon itself a voluntary Unknowledge, which by no means alters the former's nature as pure Knowledge, but brings forth a phantom universe, in which individual souls, properly one with the absolute Knowledge, imagine themselves enveloped, thus severing themselves from the latter.

Into this system Śankara interwove the chief doctrines of current Brahman orthodoxy. He himself seems to have been a Vishṇuite; his commentary on the Bhagavad-gītā asserts the supremacy of Vishṇu and the doctrine of his incarnations. But many of the religious communities claiming him as founder, and especially the Smārta Brahmans of the South, are Śaivas;

[1] It is based upon the Upanishads, Bhagavad-gītā, and Brahma-sūtra (aphorisms ascribed to Bādarāyaṇa or Vyāsa). In these texts the idea of *Māyā* is not yet developed.

and it is evident that he did good service to both these aspects of Hinduism as against the Buddhists and Jains.

Rāmānuja.—Śankara's success was enormous; but his doctrines were not without critics. The chief of these was Rāmānuja, a Tamil Brahman, born, as is usually believed, in 1127. Against Śankara's *Advaita*, or strict 'monism,' Rāmānuja set up a theory called *Viśishṭādvaita*, or 'qualified monism,' maintaining (1) that individual souls are not essentially one with the Supreme, though he is their source, and hence that the soul after salvation enters into a relation of perfect heavenly service to him, and (2) that the Supreme is not purely abstract being, but possesses real *qualities* of goodness and the like, infinite in degree. In the schools of Rāmānuja the worship of Vishṇu and his bride Lakshmī or Śrī is marked by great fervour of imagination, reminding us sometimes of Dante's visions of Paradise. There are two main divisions of the sect, *Ten-gaḷais* and *Vaḍa-gaḷais*, who differ chiefly in externals; and outside Bombay Presidency they are by far the most important representatives of Vishṇuism in the Dekkan.

Vallabhāchārya.—Another strong current of Vishṇuism arose from Vallabhāchārya, a Tailanga

Brahman, born 1478. In theory he had much affinity with Rāmānuja, but in practical religion he laid far more stress upon the myths of Kṛishṇa's childhood and amours, on which he expended the full strength of his warm and sensuous imagination. He claimed more forcibly than any other of the great Vishṇuite teachers that a god of such an attractive human personality must be worshipped by sanctifying all human pleasures to his service. This *Pushṭi-mārga*, or 'Way of Pleasure,' has naturally found many adherents, especially among the middle classes in Bombay Presidency;[1] but in practice it has lapsed into great depravity, especially as the fervour of their imagination leads devotees to dress as women, and the worshippers, regarding their *Gosains* or priests as incarnations of the god, pay to them the service which they believe to be due to him, including sometimes even the *jus primæ noctis*.

A vigorous attempt to reform this church was made in the early nineteenth century by Sahajānanda, or Svāmī Nārāyaṇa, a man of deep religious feeling and high morality, whose sect is now of some importance in Gujarat.

[1] The chief texts of the school are the Bhagavad-gītā and Bhāgavata-purāṇa.

CHAITANYA

The Eastern Revival under Chaitanya.—In 1485 was born at Nadia a Brahman who was fated to play a great part in religious history. He bore the lay names of Viśvambhara and Nīmāi, which he exchanged for that of Śrī-Kṛishṇa-Chaitanya when he took the vows in 1509.[1] In his earlier years he gained some repute as a Pandit, and showed small sympathy with the Vishṇuite church, which could hardly hold its own against the Śākta cults in Bengal and Assam. Gradually however his mind, congenitally disposed to emotional ecstasies, and indeed somewhat ill-balanced, became influenced by the *bhakti* or fervid love-service of Kṛishṇa, of which he soon came forward as chief apostle. He had no new system to propound; he was essentially a 'revivalist,' in the sense of the word familiar in England and America. He and his disciples lived as it were under a spell, possessed by an overpowering passion of love for Kṛishṇa, and dwelling ecstatically upon the forms in which the god was presented in myth. Often he would fall in a swoon of rapture. By night and day he and his congregations, to which all castes were admitted, sang hymns (*kīrttan*), shouted the

[1] Another name by which he is known in his church is *Gaurānga.*

name of Hari thousands of times,[1] danced about, and mimicked the actions of the sacred myths. From the latter form of service he developed a kind of Mystery Play, dramatically representing the legends of Kṛishṇa, either with scholastic art, as in the refined Sanskrit dramas of his disciple Rūpa Gosvāmī, or, in a more popular shape, similar to the Rās Līlā which is still performed to the rapturous delight of devout thousands. In 1533 Chaitanya disappeared. Probably he was drowned, for he had been known previously to leap into the water in a fit of ecstasy.

In so far as he was a philosopher at all, he shared the tendency of Rāmānuja and Vallabhāchārya. He held that the individual soul, typified by Kṛishṇa's mistress Rādhā, is as such not identical with the Supreme Soul, though originally it emanated thence. The Supreme Soul manifests itself personally in the universe as 'The Lord,' Kṛishṇa, and the struggles of the human soul to become united with it in the ecstasies of *bhakti* are typified in the legend of Kṛishṇa and his loves with Rādhā and the Gopīs.

In Bengal and Orissa the church of Chaitanya

[1] The simple repetition of the names *Hari* and *Kṛishṇa* is very important in the worship of this church, as a sign of grace. Many repeat them tens of thousands of times daily.

is very strong to-day. A great deal of Bengali literature is under its sway; and one who has heard at the great festival of Jagannāth at Puri the cry of *Hari bol* arising from the innumerable crowds can best appreciate the living power of the devotional passion which Chaitanya did more than any other to fan.

The Mādhva School.—We have reviewed the chief Vaishṇava sects maintaining the origin of the Soul in God; we have now to notice an important community in the Dekkan which denies this doctrine.

In 1199 was born a Brahman whose original name was Vāsudeva; when he first took the vows this was changed to *Pūrṇaprajna*, and later to *Ānanda-tīrtha*, besides which titles he is commonly known as *Madhva Āchārya*. His theory of *dvaita-vāda* or dualism maintains a real eternal distinction between the Supreme Soul, the Finite Souls, and Matter, and asserts that salvation is only possible through adoration of Vāyu, the Wind-god and son of Vishṇu, who is supposed to have been incarnated in Madhva. Unlike other teachers, who theoretically admit the possibility of any soul ultimately winning salvation, Madhva classes all souls into (1) those destined to enjoy paradise for ever when their 'works' have ceased to operate upon them, (2) those destined to everlasting rebirth, and (3) those doomed to everlasting hell. In other respects also Madhva was something of a Calvinistic reformer. In the rituals of his sect animals are never sacrificed; instead of the sheep slaughtered by their neighbours the Smārtas, the Mādhvas offer figures of dough, and their temples are not usually defiled by the ministrations of *deva-dāsīs* (official prostitutes) and *pūjārīs* (low-class priests) such as are usual elsewhere.

Other Sects.—It is impossible in this book even to enumerate all the other subdivisions of the Vishṇuites, which range from extreme sectarianism to the broadest pantheism; we give a list only of the most important.

Nimbārkas.—The sect of Nīmāvats, or Sanakādi-sampradāya, follows Nimbārka (Nimbāditya or Niyamānanda, also called Bhāskara Āchārya, perhaps of the twelfth century). They are devoted to the cult of Rādhā-Kṛishṇa, especially as conveyed in the Bhāgavata-purāṇa, and are still fairly numerous around Mathura. They are more important as a church than as a philosophical school, having little literature.

Rāmānandas.—Rāmānanda is said to have been a disciple of Rāmānuja, and seems to have borrowed some of his doctrines, but laid more stress on the cult of Rāma and Sītā. The sect, which is still numerous in Upper India, chiefly worked among the poorer classes, and its writings may almost be said to have created the Hindi literary language. It nominally rejects caste-divisions between the ascetics belonging to it.

Kabīr-panthīs.—Kabīr was a disciple of Rāmānanda, and was influenced by Islam. His sect is numerous in the North, and has penetrated also into Bombay, but has lapsed again into caste-rule, at any rate as regards the laity. Kabīr rejected idolatry and the ritual worships of Hinduism, and forbade the use of meat and strong drink. He preached a broad monistic pantheism, coloured by a warm moral fervour. God to him was the source and essence of all being, the universe his body; He brought forth Māyā, whence issued Brahma, Śiva, and Vishṇu, who by Māyā begot Sarasvatī, Umā, and Lakshmī, by whom they begot the universe. All men are alike the children of God, the manifestations of the one blessed spirit.

Nānak-panthīs.—This phase of religion may also be mentioned here, as being in origin, like the Kabīr-panth, connected on the one hand with the Vishṇuite Vedānta and on the other with Islam. Bābā Nānak (who was born in 1469 and died in 1539 near the modern town of Dera Nanak, in the Panjab,) taught the worship of a formless Supreme Being by abstract meditation, tolerance, and godliness of life. He went farther than Kabīr, for he accepted the incarnations or *avatars* and the bulk of the orthodox mythology as partially true.

To Nānak the *Sikhs* ('Disciples') owe their faith. The Nānak-panthī sect lived peacefully in the Panjab until Arjun Mall, the fifth pontiff from Nānak, was put to death by the Mughal Emperor's governor in Lahore; then they took up arms and maintained themselves in the hills of the North, where they organised themselves into a little commonwealth of Ironsides, whose hand was against Musalman and Hindu alike. Gradually their fortunes rose, and reached their zenith in the Sikh Empire of Ranjit Singh (reigned from 1799). Their chief scriptures are the Ādi Granth by Nānak and his disciples and the Das Granth by Gobind, the tenth pontiff and organiser of their military commonwealth. There are other orders also in the North and North-West which claim descent from Nānak, notably the *Nānak-shāhīs,* who are purely religious, and in some cases study philosophy also.[1]

Speaking generally, we may say that the Vishṇuite churches represent the better side of Hinduism. Some of those devoted to the cult of Kṛishṇa have however an unhappy tendency to lapse into immoral practices; and indeed it would seem that the worship of Kṛishṇa on the whole tends to put an unhealthy strain upon the emotional side of human nature, to the detriment of the moral fibre; and much of the popular worship of Vishṇu is of a commonplace and vulgar order. On the other hand, the figure of Rāma is a singularly noble and gracious ideal. All the great modern reformers, from Rāmānanda downwards, have been under its spell, and its power for good seems still to live.

Śivaite Sects.—Of the worship of Śiva it may be said at once that it has little influence for good upon the masses. Though a considerable number of the respectable middle classes worship Śiva as the supreme Being, especially in the south, most of his devotees are homeless Yogīs and similar ascetics. Perhaps the most respectable of the sectarian Śivaites are the Daṇḍīs,

[1] One of these orders has recently published two considerable Sanskrit works on philosophy ascribed to Nānak, the *Nirākāra-mīmāṃsā* and the *Adbhuta-gītā*.

Daś-nāmis, and Lingāyats. The two former are religious fraternities, chiefly ascetic, which are connected with the school of Śankara (p. 29), and are theoretically devoted to the worship and study of the Absolute Brahma, though some, at least of the Daṇḍis, sometimes lapse into more popular rites. The Lingāyats or Jangamas (Vīra-śaivas) are a puritan order of considerable importance in the South, chiefly in Mysore, who revolted from the Brahmanic supremacy and caste-rule under a certain Basava about 1165. They worship Śiva as masculine generative power, and wear the phallus as his emblem, but are generally of good repute.

The cult of Śiva affects the two poles of society. He is favoured by many high-class Brahmans and ascetics who are devoted to metaphysical studies; for the history of Śiva in this connection shows him growing from a wild mountain-devil, patron of goblins and thieves, into a mystic sorcerer-god, and thence into a type of the Yogīs (p. 24), and cognate orders of philosopher-santons. For the same reason he is popular with the lowest classes; the Yoga system in its practical side is largely based upon vulgar ideas of magic and Shamanism, and hence many of its professors have always been vulgar charlatans, and worse. These classes of devotees include fanatics who torture themselves in various ways, Aghoris, who feed on human corpses and other carrion, and Kāpālikas, who still in their disgusting rites show traces of the human sacrifices which formerly they practised. As Śiva in origin drew many of his attributes from certain barbarous aboriginal cults, so he has been at all times singularly ready to receive others into his church, especially cults involving the shedding of human blood. Moreover, Śiva's consort is chiefly worshipped under terrific forms, and her ritual also is primarily one of bloodshed.[1] Closely allied too is the Śākta movement (p. 25). These abortions of religion are in strange contrast to the higher schools of Śivaite thought, such as the mystic philosophy of the Spanda system in the North and the strange mixture of psychology and emotion which makes up the Śaiva-siddhānta of the Tamil South; but the refinements of these schools barely hide the scaffolding of savage myth on which they are built up.

The Southern devotees often rise to the highest flights of mystic rapture. Thus Māṇikka-vāśagar cries[2]:—

[1] The Thugs worshipped this goddess; but they objected to bloodshed, and throttled their victims.

[2] In Dr. Pope's edition of Māṇikka-vāśagar's *Tiruvāśagam*, pp. 72, 213. The translation is Dr. Pope's.

Sire, as in union strict, Thou mad'st me thine ; on me didst look, didst draw me near ;
And when it seemed I ne'er could be with Thee made one,—when naught of Thine was mine,—
And naught of mine was Thine,—me to thy Feet Thy love
In mystic union joined, Lord of the heavenly land !—'Tis height of blessedness !

For blessedness I seek ;—not Indra's choice delights, nor those of other gods ;—
Thou Only-One, I live not save with thy Feet twain ! Our Lord, my breast is riven,
With trembling seized ; my hands in adoration join ;
And from my eyes a ceaseless stream pours down, as of a river, O my Sage !

My sage, save to Thyself there's none to whom I cling ; in me, deceitful one,
No part from mingled falseness 'scapes ; I 'm falsehood's self ! —Partner of her whose dark
Eyes gleam, come Thou to me ! the love Thy true ones feel,—
Who at Thy jewell'd Feet in love commingling rest,—mine be it too, I pray !

I pray for love of thine own jewell'd Feet ; remove the false ; Thine own
Make me in truth ; dog though I am,—O bid me come, in grace join to Thyself,
For evermore thine own ! So let me ceaseless praise,
Thro' every world returning ever come, my King, that I may worship Thee !

And again :

The Mistress[1] dwells in midmost of Thyself ;
within the Mistress centred dwellest Thou ;
Midst of Thy servant if Ye Both do dwell,
to me Thy servant ever give the grace

[1] The *Śakti* or Cosmic Energy (p. 25).

Amidst Thy lowliest servants to abide;
 our Primal Lord, Whose being knows no end,
Who dwellest in the sacred golden porch,
 still present to fulfil my heart's intent!
* * * *

'He will not cease to pour on us His gifts,'—
 thus have I raving named Thy name,
My eyes with tears were filled,—my praising mouth
 faltered,—I bow'd,—in thought with melting soul
Many a time Thine image I recalled,
 and uttering praises named the golden court.
My Master, grant Thy grace to me, and oh!
 have pity on the soul that pines for Thee!

These great divisions, however, by no means cover the whole ground of Hindu sectarianism. There are not a few miscellaneous sects, some worshipping more or less exclusively a deity of the Brahmanic pantheon, others holding a position more or less aloof from the great standard cults which are covered by the broad mantle of orthodox Hinduism. For the latter is very catholic, and its gigantic pantheon is accepted by Vishṇuite and Śivaite alike, their differences in practice being chiefly as regards its arrangement. Every orthodox Hindu worships Gaṇeśa, the elephant-headed patron of learning and remover of hindrances, and Sūrya the Sun-god, as well as many other minor deities according to occasion or usage; and indeed one can be an orthodox Hindu without worshipping anything, provided he conform to the customs of his caste, which is really the god of many millions.

Theistic Sects of the Nineteenth Century.—Indian religion has always been subject to influences from abroad. We have seen how Islam affected minds like Kabīr and Nānak. The Christianity of the British conquerors has raised similar currents.[1]

The first and greatest of these reformers was Rāmmohan Rāy (born 1774, died 1833). He came of a good Bengali family, and zealously studied European and Semitic religious literature. In 1830 he set forth his views in a book with the suggestive title *The Precepts of Jesus the guide to peace and happiness.* Jesus he declared to be the greatest of all apostles of spiritual truths; and he read a religious meaning into the Upanishads. In 1830 too he gave practical effect to his opinions by opening a church of his own, called the *Brāhma-samāj.* This was reconstituted in 1842 by Debendranath Tagore, who declared for a kind of 'natural religion,' condemning all forms of idolatry and denying the infallibility of the Vedas. A new impulse was given to the movement in 1869 by

[1] It is often stated that King Harsha Śilāditya received Christian missionaries at his court. This is a mistake.

Keśab Chandra Sen (born 1838). The parent body was henceforth called *Ādi-Samāj*, whilst the name of *Brāhma-Samāj* was borne by the following of Keśab Chandra. From the latter branched off in 1873 the *Sādhāraṇ-samāj*, revolting from Keśab Chandra, who in his latter years became more mystical and even extravagantly ritualistic.

A similar movement produced in Bombay about 1850 the *Prārthanā-sabhā*, out of which arose in 1867 the *Prārthanā-samāj*. The latter professes unitarian doctrine and high ethical principles. It avoids Christian influences, and is chiefly inspired by the highest native intellect.

An influential school in the North and North-West is the *Ārya-samāj*, founded by Dayānanda Sarasvatī (died 1883). He professed strict monotheism, and discarded caste, traditional mythology, and orthodox idolatry. Taking up an attitude of marked hostility to Christianity, he declared that the Veda is the sole authority, and interpreted it by a most forced method of exegesis so as to justify his doctrine, even educing from it the theories of modern science. He forbade child-marriage and allowed the marriage of widows, introducing also the levirate law in certain forms.

Objects of Worship.—The vast field of Indian religion includes almost every object and mode of worship known to man. The objects are either important deities of the regular pantheon (Śiva, Vishṇu, and Brahmā,[1] with their respective consorts Pārvatī, Śrī or Lakshmī, and Sarasvatī, Rāma and Sītā, Śiva's son Skanda or Kārttikeya, the Indian Mars, Hanumān the monkey-god and ally of Rāma, the elephant-headed Gaṇeśa or Gaṇapati, who patronises learning and removes obstacles, Annapūrṇā the goddess of plenty, and many others, who are sometimes honoured with special shrines and sometimes worshipped in company with other deities), or minor gods and goddesses of the pantheon who appear only in the shrines of greater deities, or (locally) classical saints and heroes, or finally the vast and ever-increasing crowd of gods, godlings, and fetishes of all sorts whose worship arose locally outside the pale of Hinduism, but has been nominally taken under its protection, together with the various living and lifeless things appertaining to deity. 'It is not merely all the mighty phenomena and forces of the universe . . . that excite

[1] Brahmā as Demiurge is seldom worshipped exclusively. He has special shrines at Pushkar (near Ajmere), and in one or two other places.

the awe and attract the reverence of the ordinary Hindu. There is not an object in earth or heaven which he is not prepared to worship—rocks, stocks and stones, trees, pools and rivers, his own implements of trade, the animals he finds most useful, the noxious reptiles he fears, men remarkable for any extraordinary qualities—for great valour, sanctity, virtue, or even vice; good and evil demons, ghosts, and goblins, the spirits of departed ancestors, an infinite number of semi-human, semi-divine existences—inhabitants of the seven upper and the seven lower worlds—each and all of these come in for a share of divine honour or a tribute of more or less adoration.'[1]

Of the animals associated with deities, and hence included in their worship, we can notice a few only. Most important is the ox, sacred to Śiva especially, but venerated by every good Hindu. Its slaughter is a most heinous crime, and often leads to riot and bloodshed, especially between Hindus and Moslems.[2] Monkeys are sacred, because their ancestors under

[1] Monier-Williams, *Hinduism*, p. 168.

[2] When the great Śivājī wished to summon his Marathas to arms, he called upon them to protect, not their hearths and altas, but *Brahmans and cows*; and they answered the summons with enthusiasm.

Hanumān aided Rāma to overcome Rāvaṇa (p. 20); so are serpents, which are connected with the *Nāgas*, a mythological race half-human and half-serpent who dwell beneath the earth, and with Śesha, the great serpent on which Vishṇu sleeps during part of the year. Many trees also are holy—for example, the *pīpal* (*Ficus religiosa*) to Brahma, the Aśoka and Bel (*bilva, Aegle marmelos*) to Śiva, the *tulasī* or basil to Vishṇu or Kṛishṇa as his bride. Of sacred stones the most important is the *śāla-grāma* of Vishṇu, a black stone with markings similar to those of ammonites. Finally we may remark the holy places (*tīrthas*) with which India is thickly studded. The sanctity with which medieval Europe invested Jerusalem is slight in comparison with the holiness attaching to a *tīrtha*, the mere sight of which is supposed to wash away sin and secure salvation. The most famous of them is Benares (*Kāśī*), but it has many rivals, all of which energetically advertise their advantages throughout India. All the chief rivers are holy, the Ganges holiest of all;[1] and Benares is the most sacred spot on the

[1] It is accounted an act of great merit to walk from the source of a holy river down its left bank to its mouth, and thence along the right bank back to the source.

Ganges. The *tīrthas* mainly owe their existence to the ancient worship of rivers, lakes, and fountains, especially for purposes of purification; and when one spot claimed to concentrate in itself the whole sanctity of the river on which it stood, it attracted pilgrimage, and mythology developed around it. Others again have drawn their sanctity from the presence of a shrine which for some reason has become famous. Enormous numbers of pilgrims constantly visit the holy places, thus providing a livelihood for the local Brahman priests who administer for them the necessary rituals.

Forms of Worship.—The modes in which godhead is worshipped are even more manifold than the objects of worship. The ancient Brahmanic rituals were a series of immensely complicated mechanisms controlling the operations of the material universe; and by the side of these we see the doctors of the Upanishads demanding a service of abstract meditation upon Brahma (p. 15). The same opposition has always existed, even within the same church—exact ritual worship of a personal god beside *mānasa-pūjā* or mental devotion, especially to the deity in his absoluteness; and both may be performed by the same person.

The chief ceremonies of public worship are

connected with an image of the god worshipped. The image, into which the divine spirit is believed to have been introduced by the rites of inauguration, is usually treated like an honoured guest. It is washed and dressed in the morning; incense and lamps burn before it; and food is offered to it, of which the devotees partake as a Eucharist. Often, especially in the cult of Kṛishṇa, ceremonies enacting favourite myths are performed before it. To Śiva food, as a rule, is not offered. The laity most frequently offer flowers, often other things, with formal obeisances and prayers. Of the meetings for singing hymns and dancing, which are especially common among Vishṇuites, we have spoken above (p. 33).

The diversity of sects, like that of castes and occupations, is frequently shown by dress. But it is still more characteristically displayed by sectarian marks, chiefly on the forehead. Nearly every sect has a different forehead-mark, usually painted, and often also other symbols of the god stamped on the body, besides other tokens. For example, Śivaite devotees smear their bodies with the ashes of burnt cow-dung, and wear rosaries of *rudrāksha* (*eleocarpus*) berries; the more saintly they are, the less clothing they wear.

The real focus of Indian religion is in the

home. Here are performed the domestic rites on which centres the Hindu social order, the *dharma* of caste life. As these systems vary with the almost countless number of sub-castes, even an outline of them is impossible; we can give here only a brief list of the chief *saṃskāras* or lustral ceremonies and a few other rites prescribed for Brahman householders.

The *saṃskāras* consist of ceremonies previous to birth, as the *puṃsavana* or rite to ensure the birth of a son, the *sīmantonnayana* or formal parting of the hair of the wife who is about to become a mother for the first time, etc.; the rites at birth (*jāta-karma*), intended to infuse into the child strength and wisdom; the name-giving (usually two names are given, one being for ordinary use, and the other or secret name being known only to the parents, as a protection against sorcery); rites on the birth-day in every month, on the rising of the mother from her bed, on a special worship of the moon, on the first time that the child is taken into the open air, and on its first meal of solid food, all in the first year; the *chūḍākaraṇa*, usually in the third year, when the hair is cut, leaving a lock in the middle; the *keśānta* or shaving of the beard and hair, usually in the sixteenth year; the *upanayana*, when the lad is taken to a teacher and invested with the sacred cord,[1] and his religious studies are formally inaugurated; ceremonies at the beginning and end of each term of his studies; rites for the conclusion of his pupilage, when he bathes, sacrifices, and returns home; and marriage, a duty of every man, who thereby sets up a household and lights the domestic fire, in which the numerous regular sacrifices of the home are offered.

Among the chief religious duties of Brahman householders are the five *Mahā-yajnas* or 'great offerings,' viz., the *deva-yajna*, 'offering to gods,' in the household fire; the *bali-haraṇa* or *bhūta-yajna*, 'offering to the spirits,' laid in divers places for various deities; the *pitṛi-yajna*, 'offering to the Fathers' or departed ancestors; the *brahma-yajna*, 'offering to Brahma,' *i.e.* reading a Vedic text; and the *manushya-yajna*, 'offering to men,' *i.e.* hospitality to guests.

After burial the soul of the dead man remains for some months a lonely ghost, to whom sacrifices are offered (*ekoddishṭa-śrāddha*); then is

[1] This cord (*yajnopavīta*), which is hung over the left shoulder towards the right hip, is worn by the first three castes as a token of their birth; the investiture is accounted a second spiritual birth, and hence these castes are styled *dvija*, 'twice-born.'

held the rite of *sapiṇḍī-karaṇa*, by which he is united with the 'Fathers' or spirits of departed ancestors, to whom offerings (*śrāddhas*) are made by the householder and his family, both on special occasions and at regular and frequent intervals.

Principles of Caste.—The infinite variety of caste-divisions, each with a social and religious organisation of its own, arises from a number of causes. At the outset, in the Vedic period we have a simple division between the aristocratic soldier-yeoman and the priest. The former wishes to win the goodwill and active assistance of the deified powers of sky and earth in his husbandry and warfare, and to this end hires the priest, who is master of the arts of poetry and wizard rite which either cajole or constrain the invisible powers. Besides these orders there were also the elements of a trading class, *Vaiśyas*; and to these were ultimately added as lowest stratum the *Śūdras*, base-born or serfs, who included the less civilised aborigines reduced to serfdom by the Aryan invaders with perhaps a floating mass of unclassifiable population. Thus these primary 'castes' of Brahmans, Kshatriyas, Vaiśyas, and Śūdras grew up from purely social conditions; their division was accompanied by differences in religious practice, as always happens in such cases.

The next step however was fateful, and typical of Brahman thought; for the Brahmans about 800 B.C. discovered a religious and philosophic reason for these divisions. They declared that these orders represented actual divisions in Brahmā, the spirit of the Universe; the Brahmans arose from his head, the Warriors from his arms, the Vaiśyas from his thighs, and the Śūdras from his feet.[1] Thus the great social barriers were founded upon the everlasting rock of religion, to stand for all time, and the whole of the Hindu world was proclaimed one church.

The relations between the Brahmans and Kshatriyas, the head and the arm of this church, were not always very cordial. As a rule, the spiritual sovereignty was allowed to lie with the former, the temporal power with the latter. But it was not always so. Even in very early times Kshatriyas sometimes ventured to trespass upon the intellectual spheres of Brahmanism, and questioned their authority. The legend of Paraśurāma (p. 19) points to a bloody feud between the two orders; and as time went on the relative influence of the Kshatriyas declined, especially after the Muhammadan conquest. To-day there are few Kshatriyas of pure blood left in India.

[1] Ṛig-veda, x. 90.

The two lower castes naturally grew, as in them was grouped the increasing mass of population that was continually being added to this Aryan empire by conquest without or social development within, until they reached their present gigantic number. In the main a caste is a social or ethnic family with family rites and customs; its members belong together because they are of the same race or carry on the same trade, and they have an organisation of religious and social practices which binds them one with another, and sharply separates them from other castes. Even such low orders as tanners or scavengers form castes with the same close organisation and pride of class as the highest ranks of society, and would consider it a defilement to eat certain kinds of food with men of a still lower caste. The maintenance of this infinite complex constitutes what is called *dharma*, the Hindu ideal of social order and righteousness.

Retrospect.—Every great religion has borrowed some of the forms of earlier faiths. Though its central idea may be new, the historical laws of human thought demand that it be first presented in modes which shall be intelligible, and therefore not strange, to the generation which first receives it. Once accepted in these forms, it begins to develop according to its own peculiar content, and in the end may even come to cast them off as outworn trappings that check its free flight heavenward. It need therefore be no reproach to the creeds of Hinduism that they have preserved a manifold mass of ancient myths. We have rather to ask what use has been made of these crude old forms of thought, what newer ideals they have served to clothe. This question gives us the science of Hindu religion, as distinct from Hindu mythology; and Hindu religion can show glories of unsurpassed achievement. From the rudest dross of spiritual savagery in almost every field the Indian soul has again and again gathered some precious thought. It has taken from animism vague powers, from Nature in her severalty gods, from Nature in her entirety the All-God, from the heart a God of awe or love. And the forms of godhead that it has conjured up in all these domains it has bodied forth in fitting utterance; no country has a religious literature so vast and many-sided. If then we would presume to pass judgment upon the religion of India, if we would blame because so often the grossness of ancient forms has stifled the potentialities of the spirit, or because India impetuously follows every conception of heart or fancy to its uttermost bounds, even to bounds where reason faints and God Himself seems not to be, let us also remember that it has withal worthy apostles, —the nameless thinkers of the Upanishads and the Bhagavad-gītā, Tulsī Dās, the Tamil Śivaite poets, and a host of others, who bear good tidings for all time, telling in their divers voices of peace and goodwill on earth, of sanctification of every act in life to the service of the Blessed One, and of the infinite grace and wisdom which bear the worshipping soul on high to the foot of the Supreme, and even to His heart.

APPENDIX

BUDDHISM AND JAINISM[1]

Of Gautama the Śākya, called the *Buddha*, or 'Enlightened,' legend and miracle-tale speak at exuberant length. But we must pass over the truths and falsehoods of these stories; we have here to give only a broad outline of the conceptions which seem to underlie the many systems that grew up from the fertile soil of his teaching.

An atheistic, nihilistic, Hindu idealism—that is Buddhism in four words.

In principle it was not new. Such originality as it had seems to have lain in the skill of its formulæ and the august and sweet personality of its teacher. He taught the law of virtue, the sin of taking life; he led an opposition against the Brahmanic papacy and threw open the gate of salvation to all castes. What was boldest of all, he utterly denied the existence of soul or spirit, the *ātmā* of orthodox philosophy.

Buddhism as a system of thought is based upon two formulæ, the 'Noble Truths' (*ārya-satyāni*) and the twelvefold 'Causal Evolution' (*pratītya-samutpāda*).

[1] A special volume in this series is devoted to Buddhism; it is therefore necessary only to sketch its outline.

BUDDHISM

The Noble Truths are the facts of 'pain, cause, suppression, and way'; that is to say, life is essentially sorrow, which arises from a cause, from the diagnosis of which one may learn the method to heal the sorrow. The method is the Law of the Buddha, leading to *Nirvāṇa*, the peace that passes all understanding.

The 'Causal Evolution' analyses the process by which the individual who is the subject of thought —in other words, the conscious Idea—arises from the void of Being, the unconscious All or All-Idea. From 'Ignorance' are born 'Conformations' (*saṃskāras*), indeterminate sense-impressions; thence arises *vijnāna*, determinate consciousness; thence 'Name-and-Form,' the individual subject compounded of feeling, sense-impressions, specific notion, and determinate consciousness allied with matter; thence the six organs of sense; thence the contact of the organs with their objects without; thence blind feeling; thence desire; thence a clinging to the phantoms of consciousness; thence the beginning of bodied life; thence birth; and thence the circumstances of life, age and death, grief and pain, amidst which the cycle ends, only to begin anew.

If we ask what is the cause of these innumerable processions of ideas from unconsciousness towards consciousness, the Buddhist replies that it is 'Works,' *Karma*. But according to the other Indian schools 'Works' must be attached to an *ātmā*, a permanent individuality or Soul, in which proceed all phaenomenal processes such as those of the 'Causal Evolution'; and Buddhism denies *ātmā*. How then can 'Works' operate where there is no *ātmā*? The Buddhist's answer is that the whole course of existence, both of the subject and of the world, is a series of momentary states of consciousness, each of which is the direct resultant of those that have gone before it; and it is in these successive phases that 'Work' realises itself. When one group of physical elements is worn out and death occurs, the 'work' resulting from the previous series of consciousness at once creates from the void of Being a new group in this or that sphere, and the process goes on anew. But it does not always go on for ever. It may happen to some that the energy of their 'Works' grows less and less, and is at last dissipated for ever by the Good Law, by spiritual exercises and ascetic mortification; and then they will be born never again, for they have won *nirvāṇa*, the 'extinction' of the power that leads to birth, and when they die they come to everlasting *parinirvāṇa*, perfect extinction, the supreme Good. Logically this state of extinction means the absolute negation of all conditioned existence for ever; practically it signifies to most Buddhists everlasting supernal bliss.

Jainism appears to have arisen a little earlier in the sixth century B.C. than Buddhism, and was part of the same general movement. Its leader was Mahāvīra or Vardhamāna, who like the Buddha was of an aristocratic family of Eastern India, and claimed to bear the mantle of earlier teachers.

The scaffolding upon which Jainism has built up its clumsy and mechanical system is summed up in the formula of the 'Nine Realities' (*tattva*), namely, 'Soul, Non-soul, Influx, Exclusion, Dissipation, Imprisonment, Release, Merit, Sin.' There are infinitely many souls (*jīva*) in the universe, wandering from birth to birth. Their ideal function is perfect and unconditioned knowledge of the truth of being, in a state of freedom from all influences whatsoever, and to this they attain if they become 'released' for ever. But during life the souls of all but the most exalted saints suffer the 'influx' (*āsrava*), influences of mental frailty, which rivet the mechanical bonds of 'Works' upon them, whence they are driven to continued actions either meritorious or sinful in bodied life. With religious exercises, virtue, and mortifications these fetters can be loosened, and prevented from forming again.

In their conceptions of soul the Jains are most primitive and most consistent. Souls in bodied existence they classify as either immobile or mobile. The immobile compose earth, water, fire, wind or air, and vegetation; all these are made up of tiny soul-bodies, which must not be wilfully harmed. Mobile souls are those that inspire all the other phases of life. All souls are of limited dimension in space. Opposed to soul is non-soul or inanimate Matter, the medium in which souls move in their wanderings, and which inspires in them the sense-impressions in which their 'Works' manifest themselves to them. A supreme World-god is admitted, but his prerogatives are jealously limited; practically he represents nothing more than the total energy of cosmic Matter. The various gods of the Hindu pantheon appear on the stage of Jainism; but they are merely souls whose meritorious works have raised them for a time to higher bliss, as in Buddhism also. But even a Jain or a Buddhist must have something to worship. The Buddhists of the North worship their master as a living god, those of the South adore him as the guide who has gone before. The Jains, in their turn, pay a service of intense devotion and true *bhakti* not only to Mahāvīra but also to the twenty-three other 'Makers of the Passage' (*tīrthaṃkara*) or 'Conquerors' (*Jina*) from whose spiritual lineage he claimed to have arisen.

In other respects, too, the Jains go further than Buddhism, which was essentially a *via media*. As they find soul in many more things, they are forced to be far more heedful to avoid harming it. So in their nervous carefulness they have created a system which is perfectly grotesque. An orthodox monk dare not eat even green vegetables or such as contain seeds; during the rains he must sit still, and in travelling at any time he must carefully observe the ground in front of him, for fear of treading upon any vermin or even lower forms of life, and if he sees any such he gently sweeps them away with the brush that he carries.[1] The laity, of course, are not bound by all the details of this discipline; most vegetables are permitted to them. They live under a reasonably strict code of morals, with frequent spiritual exercises and fasts; and their tenderness for animal life finds practical expression in maintaining hospitals for beasts.

Buddhism looked forward to death; Jainism anticipated it. Its dreary scriptures are crowded with tales

[1] We find this morbid tenderness elsewhere; *e.g.* it is said of a diseased disciple of Chaitanya that when the vermin dropped from his sores he gently replaced them.

of enthusiasts who hastened their souls' release by systematic starvation; and in history this ideal has been abundantly realised. In the days when the religion was flourishing, thousands of devotees starved themselves to death in sacred places such as Sravana Belgole.

The Jain community is still very important in Marwar, Bombay Presidency, and Mysore, where it includes a considerable proportion of the respectable middle classes, especially the merchants. In spite of its crassly mechanical doctrine and dull scholasticism, it has produced a large literature of a high order, in which there are many works that will bear comparison with the best of Hindu writings.

HISTORICAL SUMMARY

I. The Vedic age, dominated by polytheism and animism. The gods of the former class are nature-powers cast more or less completely into human form and surrounded by myth and saga; their figures gradually tend to melt one into another, and thus the soil is prepared for Pantheism.

II. The age of the Brāhmaṇas and Upanishads, about 800-600 B.C. On the one hand, personal worship gives way to ecclesiastical ritualism on a gigantic scale. On the other hand, but often in the same persons, the theory of Upanishadic Pantheism arises; all is essentially the One, Brahma, which is at once the Cosmic and the Absolute Idea. The older gods, as cosmic phaenomena, are subordinated to Brahma. The popular faith however remains primarily Vedic. Vishṇu and Śiva rise in estimation, and gradually win recognition as representatives of the Absolute.

III. From about the sixth century onwards there are local revolts of the laity against Brahmanic sovereignty, notably Buddhism and Jainism. These movements tend to reject a personal supreme god, to break down caste barriers, to lay great stress on mercy towards all living things, to hold out the hope of salvation by works and faith, and to worship their teachers. Brahmanism, finally victorious, learns from them to spare life. For its popular propaganda the Purāṇas begin to appear. The worship of the Cosmic Energy as female counterpart to the deity (Śākta and Tantric cults) is definitively established.

IV. From the tenth century onwards a new intellectual reform of Brahmanism is noticeable (Śankara, Rāmānuja, etc.). Vishṇuism develops further its emotional and romantic side by paying special attention to the legends of Kṛishṇa's birth, childhood, and pastoral amours. Śivaism takes a strong hold of the intellect and heart of the Tamils.

V. From the eleventh century (the Muhammadan conquest), sects begin to arise with a tendency towards monotheism, similar to the Muslim orders.

SELECTED WORKS BEARING UPON HINDU RELIGION

TREATISES

The Religions of India, by A. Barth.
Indian Wisdom, by Sir Monier Williams.
The Religions of India, by E. W. Hopkins.
Asiatic Studies, by Sir A. C. Lyall.
The Hindu Pantheon, by E. Moor.
Hindu Mythology, by J. Dowson.
Hinduism, by Sir Monier Williams.
Vedic Mythology, by A. A. Macdonell (in Buehler's *Grundriss der indo-arischen Philologie und Altertumskunde*).
The Atharvaveda, by M. Bloomfield (same series).

TRANSLATIONS

The Sacred Books of the East (several volumes of this collection are translations from Veda, Brāhmaṇas, Upanishads, and Mahābhārata).
The Wealth of the East, edited by Manmatha Nath Datt (contains several Purāṇas, Tantras, etc.).
Ṛig-veda, translated by R. T. H. Griffith.
Sechzig Upanishad's des Veda, translated by P. Deussen.
Mahābhārata, edited by Protap Chandra Roy.
Rāmāyaṇa, translated by R. T. H. Griffith.
Tiru-vāçagam of Māṇikka-vāçagar, edited and translated by G. U. Pope.
Bhagavad-gītā (Temple Classics).
Rāmāyaṇa of Tulsī Dās, translated by F. S. Growse.